P9-BHW-643

What Others Are Saying about this Book

The Attitude Treasury is a unique and powerful collection of quotations. Some will make you smile, others will bring a tear—but all are inspiring. Certainly, this book would be a sterling addition to your personal library.
Diane de Porter, Free-lance Writer

These ideas will help you renew your inner strength.
Billy Mills, Olympic Gold Medallist,
Author and Motivational Speaker

Marty has done a masterful job of selecting and organizing inspirational messages for "uplifting results." Rob Scherer, President
R. M. Scherer & Associates
presenting Dale Carnegie Training®

These beautiful quotations offer answers for any concern you might have. I recommend a copy on every nightstand for early morning or late evening inspiration. Jane Nelsen, Ed.D.
Author, Counselor and Motivational Speaker

Tom Peters showed us where to go—*The Attitude Treasury* keeps us going there. A must for any executive's desk. Steve Beede, Broker/Investor

Inspiration, enthusiasm, and determination are all by-products of a positive attitude. This book will help you maintain that attitude.
Burl W. Waits, Attorney and Founder
The Foundation to Promote Positive Learning Processes

This book is bursting with positive thoughts: encouraging, joyful, energizing. You'll open it often, and you'll always be uplifted when you do.
Sandra Hinks, Free-lance Writer

An inspiring book for all persons, for all seasons!
Alan Schonberg
President, Management Recruiters International

The Attitude Treasury will have a place of honor in each room to inspire and uplift our guests.
Marlene Cartwright
High Country Inn B&B, Sierra City, CA

A celebration of life. You'll discover more of yourself in these bits of wisdom.
Jean Dunham, Real Estate Broker

A gentle, heartwarming book that truly brings out the beauty of the human spirit.
Nancy Bushey, Motivational Speaker

A valuable compendium on how to be happy.
Ernest Hartley, Director, Towe Ford Museum

This book is inspirational and well-organized.
John K. Silberman
Vice President, Telos Corporation

The Attitude Treasury reaches within me, draws out half-remembered truths, and inspires me once again.
Doug Thompson
Director of Finance, Port of Sacramento

You can use this book for inspiration, for thinking, for quoting—but for goodness sake, use it!
Marj Stuart, Writing Consultant

The Attitude Treasury is a companion to inspire and instruct—a book that brings out our higher selves.
Clay Sigg, Managing Broker, Lyon & Associates

This wonderful collection alternately inspires, soothes, and warms the heart. It's a treasure.
Lila L. Anastas, Author, *Listen to Your Body*

The Attitude Treasury
101 Inspiring Quotations

Edited by Marty Maskall

Foreword by Barbara Pletcher

The Attitude Works Publishing Company
Fair Oaks, California

The Attitude Treasury
101 Inspiring Quotations

Edited by Marty Maskall

Published by:
   The Attitude Works Publishing Company
   8456 Hidden Valley Circle
   Fair Oaks, CA 95628
   916/967-2470

Publisher's Cataloging in Publication Data

The Attitude Treasury: 101 Inspiring Quotations /
edited by Marty Maskall; foreword by Barbara
Pletcher. --
   p. cm.
   Includes bibliographical references and indexes.

1. Quotations, English   I. Maskall, Marty, 1945-

PN6081   080   LC 90-84617
ISBN 0-9627670-2-6 $9.95 Softcover

This book is for you, dear reader.

May these ideas inspire you as much as they have inspired me.

Acknowledgments

This book was inspired by my many positive-thinking friends over the years, and particularly by my mother who taught me to love words and their power. I am especially grateful to my friends in Toastmasters International, who have given me encouragement and support. I am also indebted to Ruth Cleary, Vineeta Chand, Tillie Maskall, Virginia Stellmach, Marj Stuart, Nancy Bushey, Kristy Hartley, Ernie Hartley, Helen Daley, Gayle De Forest, Steve Beede, Phil Hoover, Sid Gesh, Lynn Walker, Bud Gardner, Rich Armentrout and Marlene Cartwright for valuable suggestions.

The original authors of the quotations included here are listed in the bibliography. If no author is indicated in the text, it is because the source could not be determined. The editor gratefully acknowledges the contribution of all other authors—known and unknown.

The beautiful illustrations are taken from Charlene Tarbox's *Floral Designs* book, which is also listed in the bibliography.

Table of Contents

Foreword

When faced with an opportunity, some people grasp it and make the most of it; others shrink back and doubt their abilities.

When hit with a disappointment, some people pick themselves up and make the best of it; others sit down and give up.

When grief strikes, some people are able to convert those sad feelings into positive energy and move on with life; others wallow in self-pity.

What makes the difference? *Attitude*.

With the right attitude you can accomplish almost anything, and you'll enjoy yourself more as you take on life's challenges or face those frustrations and aggravations that we all share.

When Marty Maskall told me she was compiling a collection of 101 inspiring quotations, my first thought was "If anyone can pick the winners, Marty can." Marty's entire life is a testimony to the wisdom of cultivating your attitude so that you are prepared to make the most of your life.

This book can change your life. It's a resource, a tool. When you feel doubtful, pick it up and turn to the section *Courageous Expressions*. You'll find a thought that will restore your sense of self-worth. When you feel sad, turn to *Happy Thoughts* and pick up your spirits. Grief, frustration, aggravation, disappointment, failure, or just plain lethargy—there's a quotation in this book that will hit the spot.

With this book you can help others improve their lives, too. How many times have you wished that you had just the right thought to share with a friend or relative in a time of need? Those right thoughts are in this collection. When you send that next graduation present, wedding gift, or sympathy note, you'll feel good about selecting one of these messages to share.

I am absolutely certain that you'll treasure *The Attitude Treasury*.

Barbara Pletcher, DBA
Founder,
National Association for Professional Saleswomen
Sacramento, California

Preface

I hope you will enjoy reading this book as much I have enjoyed creating it. Though we may never meet in person, we share the bond formed by these beautiful ideas.

The title, *The Attitude Treasury*, reflects my belief in the importance of a good attitude. For many years I have maintained that there is no problem that cannot be solved, or at least made more manageable, by an ice cream cone. This book is designed to be an ice cream cone for your mind. Its purpose is to recharge your batteries and to create a smile in your soul.

I focus on attitude because, with the right attitude, life's challenges are much easier to tackle. It is tempting to let our attitude droop when we are bombarded with the many negative messages all around us. I hope this book will become your friend and your personal antidote to negative thinking.

I have taken the liberty of rewording some passages in order to avoid sexist language—for example, Rudyard Kipling's poem *If*. I hope that female readers appreciate the difference and that male readers understand and appreciate the spirit of the change.

The selections have been chosen from inspiring passages which I have collected over the years. The 101 quotations have been arranged in eight groupings for easy reference:

Happy Thoughts—
        to brighten your heart
Positive Attitudes—
        to strengthen motivation
Courageous Expressions—
        for reinforcement
Wise Words—
        common sense to heed and share
Reflections on Success—
        for goals and balance
Guidance—
        for reassurance
Spiritual Sayings—
        to nurture your soul
Rewards—
        for a job well done

Whenever you pick up this book, I hope that it will add sunshine to your life.

Read and enjoy!

        Marty Maskall
        October 1, 1990
        Fair Oaks, California

Happy Thoughts

Happiness

Happiness is a butterfly,
    which when pursued
    is always just beyond your grasp,
But which,
    if you will sit down quietly,
    may alight upon you.

❧ NATHANIEL HAWTHORNE

A Host of Golden Daffodils

I wandered lonely as a cloud
That floats on high o'er vales and hills,
When all at once I saw a crowd,
A host, of golden daffodils;
Beside the lake, beneath the trees,
Fluttering and dancing in the breeze.
Continuous as the stars that shine
And twinkle on the milky way,
They stretched in never-ending line
Along the margin of a bay.

Ten thousand saw I at a glance,
Tossing their heads in sprightly dance.
The waves beside them danced; but they
Outdid the sparkling waves in glee.
A poet could not but be gay,
In such a jocund company.
I gazed—and gazed—but little thought
What wealth the show to me had brought:

For oft, when on my couch I lie
In vacant or in pensive mood,
They flash upon that inward eye
Which is the bliss of solitude;
And then my heart with pleasure fills,
And dances with the daffodils.

ॐ WILLIAM WORDSWORTH

3

Do Not Fear Tomorrow

I do not fear tomorrow,

    for I have seen yesterday,

        and I love today.

ଛଲ WILLIAM ALLEN WHITE

Action and Happiness

Action may not always
   bring happiness;

But there is no happiness
   without action.

ଛଲ BENJAMIN DISRAELI

A Smile

A smile costs nothing, but gives much.
It enriches those who receive, without
    making poorer those who give.
It takes but a moment, but the memory
    of it sometimes lasts forever.

None are so rich or mighty that
    they can get along without it,
    and none are so poor but that
    they can be made rich by it.
A smile creates happiness in the home,
    fosters good will in business,
    and is the countersign of friendship.

It brings rest to the weary,
    cheer to the discouraged,
    sunshine to the sad,
    and it is nature's best antidote for trouble.

Yet it cannot be bought, begged, borrowed,
    or stolen, for it is something that is of
    no value to anyone until it is given away.

Some people are too tired
    to give you a smile.
Give them one of yours,
    as no one needs a smile so much
    as one who has none left to give.

                          ❧ FRANK IRVING FLETCHER

Don't Walk in Front of Me

Don't walk in front of me...
    I may not follow.

Don't walk behind me...
    I might not lead.

Just walk beside me
    and be my friend.

Friendship Improves Happiness

Friendship improves happiness,
    and abates misery,
        by doubling our joy, and
        dividing our grief.

                                JOSEPH ADDISON

A Friend

Those who have a thousand friends
Have not a friend to spare.

But those who have enemies
    Shall meet them everywhere.

A friend is one who knows you as you are,
    Understands where you've been,
    Accepts who you've become,
    And still gently invites you to grow.

Change

Consider how hard it is
    to change yourself, and
You'll understand
    what little chance you have of
    trying to change others.

&❧ JACOB M. BRAUDE

If You Want Happiness

If you want happiness for an hour—
    take a nap.
If you want happiness for a day—
    go fishing.
If you want happiness for a month—
    get married.
If you want happiness for a year—
    inherit a fortune.
If you want happiness for a lifetime—
    help someone else.

❧ CHINESE PROVERB

Through the Eyes of Children

Through the eyes of children,
The world seems bright and gay.
The misgivings of our society
Seem to drift away.

Through children's eyes, we aren't judged
By the color of our skin,
But by the way we act and conduct ourselves
And the qualities within.

A child sees the simple things
That we pass by each day,
And views them with wonderment
In a very special way.

If only we could view the world
The way that children see,
We could reach and touch the souls
                Of all humanity.

Recipe for Happiness

The chief thing you are seeking
in this world is happpiness;
and happiness does not depend on
good health or money or fame,
though good health is a large factor.

It depends, however, principally on
one thing only: your thoughts.
If you can't have what you want,
be grateful for what you have.

Keep thinking constantly of all
the big things you have to be thankful for
instead of complaining about
the little things that annoy you.

&ª DALE CARNEGIE

Positive Attitudes

The Magic Word, Attitude

* It is our attitude at the beginning of a task which, more than anything else, will effect its successful outcome.

* It is our attitude towards life which determines life's attitude toward us.

* We are interdependent. It is impossible to succeed without others, and it is our attitude towards others which will determine their attitude toward us.

* Before you can achieve the kind of life you want, you must become that kind of individual. You must act, think, talk, walk, and conduct yourself in all your affairs as would that individual.

* The higher you go in any organization of value, the better will be the attitude you will find.

* Your mind can hold only one thought at a time, and since there is nothing to be gained by being negative, be positive.

* The deepest craving of human beings is to be needed, to feel important, to be appreciated. Give these gifts to them, and they will return them to you.

* Look for the best in new ideas. As someone said, "I've never met a person I couldn't learn something from."

* Don't waste valuable time broadcasting personal problems. It probably won't help you, and it cannot help others.

* Don't talk about your health unless it's good.

* Radiate the attitude of well-being, of confidence, of knowing where you are going. This will *inspire* those around you, and you will find good things happening to you.

* For the next thirty days, treat everyone with whom you come into contact as the most important person in the world!

Attitude

The Most Powerful Thing You Can Do

The most powerful thing you can do
    to change the world,
Is to change your own beliefs
    about the nature of life, people, reality,
To something more positive...

And begin to act accordingly.

                            ❧ SHAKTI GAWAIN

Look to This Day

Listen to the exhortation of the dawn!

Look to this day!
For it is life, the very life of life.
In its brief course lie all the
realities and truths of your existence:
    The bliss of growth,
    The glory of action,
    The splendor of beauty.

For yesterday is but a dream,
And tomorrow is only a vision.
But today, well lived, makes
    Every yesterday a dream of happiness and
    Every tomorrow a vision of hope.

Look well, therefore, to this day!
Such is the salutation of the dawn.

                           ᐧ KALIDASA

My World—My Attitude

My world is

a reflection

of my attitude.

Don't Wait for Your Ship

Don't wait for your ship to come in.

Swim out to it.

The Optimist Creed

Promise yourself:

* To be so strong that nothing can disturb your peace of mind.
* To talk health, happiness and prosperity to everyone you meet.
* To make all your friends feel that there is something in them.
* To look at the sunny side of everything and make your optimism come true.
* To think only of the best, to work only for the best, and to expect only the best.
* To be just as enthusiastic about the success of others as you are about your own.
* To forget the mistakes of the past and press on to the greater achievements of the future.
* To wear a friendly countenance at all possible times and give every living creature you meet a smile.
* To spend so much time in improving yourself that you have no time to criticize others.
* To be too large for worry, too noble for anger, too strong for fear, and too happy to permit the presence of trouble.

ॐ OPTIMIST INTERNATIONAL

17

I Never Knew a Night So Black

I never knew a night so black
Light failed to follow on its track.

I never knew a storm so gray,
It failed to have its clearing day.

I never knew such bleak despair,
That there was not a rift, somewhere.

I never knew an hour so drear,
Love could not fill it full of cheer.

People—Love Them Anyway

People are unreasonable,
illogical and self-centered.
    Love them anyway.

If you do good, people will
accuse you of ulterior motives.
    Do good anyway.

If you are successful, you win
false friends and true enemies.
    Succeed anyway.

The good you do today
will be forgotten tomorrow.
    Do good anyway.

Honesty and frankness
make you vulnerable.
    Be honest and frank anyway.

What you spend years building
may be destroyed overnight.
    Build anyway.

People really need help, but
may attack you if you help them.
    Help people anyway.

Give the world the best you have
and you may get kicked in the teeth.
    Give the world your best anyway.

Today's Opportunity

Between
   tomorrow's dream and
      yesterday's regret, is
         today's opportunity.

When You Are Inspired

When you are inspired by some great
purpose, some extraordinary project,
all your thoughts break their bonds;

Your mind transcends limitations,
your consciousness expands
in every direction,
and you find yourself in a new,
great and wonderful world.

Dormant forces, faculties and talents
become alive, and you discover yourself
to be a greater person by far than
you ever dreamed yourself to be.

                                               ❧ PATANJALI

Set Your Sights High

Set your sights high,
    the higher the better.

Expect the most wonderful things
    to happen, not in the future
        but right now.

Realize that nothing is too good.

Allow absolutely nothing
    to hamper you
        or hold you up
            in any way.

ಶ EILEEN CADDY

Climb the Mountains

Climb the mountains and
    get their good tidings.
        Nature's peace will flow into you
            as sunshine flows into the trees.

The winds will blow
    their own freshness into you,
        and the storms their energy,
            while your cares will drop off
                like autumn leaves.

                      JOHN MUIR

Ten Attitude Commandments

1. It is attitude, not aptitude, that governs altitude.

2. The purpose of existence is not to make a living, but to make a life.

3. A negative thought is a down payment on an obligation to fail.

4. You will seldom experience regret for anything you've done. It's what you don't do that will torment you.

5. Complaining is the refuge of those who have no self-reliance.

6. The ultimate cost of something is that amount of life that you will exchange for it.

7. Youth is not a time of life, but a state of mind. Wrinkles test the skin, but never touch the soul.

8. People who have not set a worthwhile purpose in life are easy prey for anxiety.

9. The worst bankruptcy is the person who has lost enthusiasm.

10. Nobody can make you feel inferior without your consent.

Courageous
Expressions

No Longer Afraid

And only when we are no longer afraid
    do we begin to live in every experience,
    painful or joyous:

To live in gratitude for every moment,
    to live abundantly.

              ಎ DOROTHY THOMPSON

A Foolish Consistency

A foolish consistency is the
     hobgoblin of little minds...
With consistency a great soul
     has simply nothing to do.
You may as well concern yourself with
     your shadow on the wall.

Speak what you think now in hard words,
     and tomorrow speak what you think
     tomorrow in hard words again,
     though it contradict everything
     you said today.
"Ah, so you shall be sure
     to be misunderstood."

Is it so bad, then, to be misunderstood?
Pythagoras was misunderstood, and Socrates,
and Jesus, and Luther, and Copernicus, and
Galileo, and Newton, and every pure and
wise spirit that ever took flesh.

To be great is to be misunderstood.

                        ≈ RALPH WALDO EMERSON

The Journey of a Thousand Miles

The journey
    of a thousand miles
        begins and ends
            with one step.

ぞ LAO TSU

One Person with Courage

One person with
    courage
        makes a
            majority.

ぞ ANDREW JACKSON

Risk

To laugh is to risk appearing a fool.
To weep is to risk appearing sentimental.
To reach out to another
     is to risk involvement.
To expose feelings is to risk rejection.
To place your dreams before the crowd
     is to risk ridicule.
To love is to risk not being loved in return.
To live is to risk dying.
To hope is to risk despair.
To try is to risk failure.

But risks must be taken;
Because the greatest hazard in life
     is to risk nothing.
People who risk nothing, do nothing,
     have nothing, and are nothing.
They may avoid suffering and sorrow,
     but they cannot learn, feel,
     change, grow, or love.

Only a person who risks is free.

Just for Today

Just for today:

*   I will try to be happy. Abraham Lincoln said, "Most folks are about as happy as they make up their minds to be." He was right. I will not dwell on thoughts that depress me. I will chase them out of my mind and replace them with happy thoughts.

*   I will try to adjust myself to what is, and not try to adjust everything to my own desires. I will take my family, my business, and my luck as they come and fit myself to them.

*   I will take care of my body. I will exercise it, care for it, nourish it, not abuse it nor neglect it, so that it will be a perfect machine for my bidding.

*   I will try to strengthen my mind. I will learn something useful. I will not be a mental loafer. I will read something that requires effort, thought and concentration.

*   I will exercise my soul in three ways. I will do somebody a good turn and not get found out. I will do at least two things I don't want to do just for exercise.

*   I will be agreeable. I will look as well as I can, dress becomingly, talk softly, act courteously, be liberal with praise, speak ill of no one, and not try to improve anybody except myself.

*   I will try to live through this day only, not to tackle my whole life problem at once. I can do things for twelve hours that would appall me if I had to keep them up for a lifetime.

*   I will have a program. I may not follow it exactly, but I will have it, thereby saving myself from two pests, hurry and indecision.

*   I will have a quiet half hour to relax alone. During this time, I will reflect on my behavior and will try to get a better perspective on my life.

*   I will be unafraid. I will gather the courage to do what is right and take the responsibility for my own actions. I will expect nothing from the world, but I will realize that as I give to the world, the world will give to me.

🙷 SYBYL PARTRIDGE AND ALCOHOLICS ANONYMOUS

Be Not the Slave of Your Own Past

Be not the slave of your own past—
    plunge into the sublime seas,
    dive deep, and swim far,
So you shall come back with self respect,
    with new power,
    with an advanced experience,
That shall explain and overlook the old.

                         ᐓ RALPH WALDO EMERSON

We Never Know How High We Are

We never know how high we are
Till we are called to rise;
And then, if we are true to plan,
Our statures touch the skies.

The heroism we recite
Would be a daily thing,
Did not ourselves the cubits warp
For fear to be a king.

                           ᐓ EMILY DICKINSON

Do Not Be Too Timid

Do not be too timid and squeamish
    about your actions.
All life is an experiment.
The more experiments you make, the better.
What if they are a little coarse,
    and you may get your coat soiled or torn?

What if you do fail, and get fairly
    rolled in the dirt once or twice?

Up again,
    you shall never be so afraid of a tumble.

                                   ❧ RALPH WALDO EMERSON

You Must Do the Thing

You gain strength, courage and confidence
    by every experience
    in which you must stop and
    look fear in the face...

You must do the thing
you think you cannot do.

                                   ❧ ELEANOR ROOSEVELT

Some People See Things

Some people see things
as they are and say

    "Why?"

I dream things
that never were, and say,

    "Why not?"

                                         ❧ GEORGE BERNARD SHAW

Wise Words

Chance Favors

Chance favors
   the prepared mind.

                                    ❧ LOUIS PASTEUR

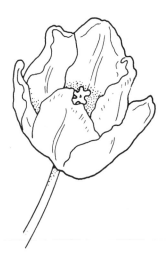

Believe in Yourself

Believe in yourself, and in your dreams,
    though impossible things may seem.
Someday, somehow you'll get through
    to that goal you have in view.

Mountains fall and seas divide
    before the ones who, in their stride,
Take a hard road, day by day,
    sweeping life's obstacles away.

Believe in yourself and in your plan.
    Say not, I cannot, but I can!
The prizes of life we fail to win,
    because we doubt the power within.

                                  ε℀ BRIAN C. HOLZ

Do the Hard Jobs First

Do the hard jobs first.

The easy jobs will
    take care of themselves.

&> DALE CARNEGIE

Genius and Perspiration

Genius
    is one percent
            inspiration
    and
        ninety-nine percent
            perspiration.

&> THOMAS A. EDISON

Never Become Discouraged

I never allow myself to become discouraged
under any circumstances...

The three great essentials to achieve
anything worthwhile are:
    Hard work,
    Stick-to-itiveness, and
    Common sense.

❀ THOMAS A. EDISON

Obstacles

Obstacles are
    what you see
        when you take your eyes off
            your goal.

I Shall Not Pass This Way Again

I shall pass
        through this world but once.

Any good that I can do,
Or any kindness that I can show,
Let me not defer nor neglect it.

For I shall not pass this way again.

There Is Only a Slight Difference

There is only a slight difference
        between keeping your chin up and
                sticking your neck out,
but it's worth knowing.

Life Is the Movie You See

Life is the movie you see
   through your own, unique eyes.

It makes little difference
   what's happening out there.

It's how *you* take it that counts.

&❧ DENIS WAITLEY

Problems Are Opportunities

Problems
   are only opportunities
      in work clothes.

&❧ HENRY J. KAISER

All I Really Need to Know
I Learned in Kindergarten

All I really need to know about how to live and what to do and how to be I learned in kindergarten. Wisdom was not at the top of the graduate-school mountain, but there in the sandpile at Sunday School. These are the things I learned:

> Share everything.
> Play fair.
> Don't hit people.
> Put things back where you found them.
> Clean up your own mess.
> Don't take things that aren't yours.
> Say you're sorry when you hurt someone.
> Wash your hands before you eat.
> Flush.

Warm cookies and cold milk are good for you. Live a balanced life—learn some and think some and draw and paint and sing and dance and play and work every day some.

Take a nap every afternoon. When you go out into the world, watch out for traffic, hold hands and stick together.

Be aware of wonder. Remember the little seed in the Styrofoam cup: The roots go down and the plant goes up and nobody really knows how or why, but we are all like that.

Goldfish and hamsters and white mice and even the little seed in the Styrofoam cup—they all die. So do we.

And then remember the Dick-and-Jane books and the first word you learned—the biggest word of all—LOOK.

Everything you need to know is in there somewhere. The Golden Rule and love and basic sanitation. Ecology and politics and equality and sane living.

Take any one of those items and extrapolate it into sophisticated adult terms and apply it to your family life or your work or your government or your world and it holds true and clear and firm. Think what a better world it would be if we all—the whole world—had cookies and milk about three o'clock every afternoon and then lay down with our blankies for a nap. Or if all governments had a basic policy to always put things back where they found them and to clean up their own mess.

And it is still true, no matter how old you are—when you go out into the world, it is best to hold hands and stick together.

&. ROBERT FULGHUM

Things May Come

Things may come to
   those who wait,

But only the things left
   by those who hustle.

&. ABRAHAM LINCOLN

Truth Has No Special Time

Truth has no special time
   of its own.

Its hour is now—
   always.

&. ALBERT SCHWEITZER

Yesterday, Tomorrow, Today

Yesterday is a cancelled check;
Tomorrow is a promissory note;
Today is the only cash you have—
So spend it wisely.

&. KAY LYONS

Reflections on Success

Accept Only the Best

It is a funny thing about life;

If you refuse to accept anything
   but the best,
   you very often get it.

≥∿ SOMERSET MAUGHAM

To Be Successful

To be successful
   is to achieve an objective,

but to be a success
   is always to have yet another objective
   in mind after you've achieved the last one.

Commitment

Until one is committed, there is hesitancy, the chance to draw back, always ineffectiveness.

Concerning all acts of initiative (and creation), there is one elementary truth, the ignorance of which kills countless ideas and splendid plans:

That the moment one definitely commits oneself, then Providence moves too.

All sorts of things occur to help one that would never otherwise have occurred. A whole stream of events issues from the decision, raising in one's favor all manner of unforeseen incidents and meetings and material assistance, which no one could have dreamed would have come their way.

Whatever you can do or dream you can,
    begin it.
Boldness has genius, magic and power in it.
    Begin it now.

ﻥ JOHANN WOLFGANG GOETHE

Castles in the Air

If you advance confidently in the
    direction of your dreams and
    endeavor to live the life which
    you have imagined,
You will meet with a success
    unexpected in common hours...

If you have built castles in the air,
    your work need not be lost;
    that is where they should be.

Now put the foundations under them.

ە HENRY DAVID THOREAU

It Is Not the Critic Who Counts

It is not the critic who counts, not the one who points out how a strong person stumbled, or where the doer of deeds could have done them better.

The credit belongs to those who are actually in the arena; whose faces are marred by dust and sweat and blood; who strive valiantly, who err and come short again and again; who know the great enthusiasms, the great devotions, and spend themselves in a worthy cause;

Who, at the best, know in the end the triumph of high achievement; and who, at the worst, if they fail, at least fail while daring greatly, so that their place shall never be with those cold and timid souls who know neither victory nor defeat.

                            ও THEODORE ROOSEVELT

The Impossible

It is difficult to say
    what is impossible,

For the dream of yesterday
    is the hope of today
        and the reality of tomorrow.

჆ ROBERT H. GODDARD

What Is Hustle?

Hustle is doing something that everyone is absolutely certain can't be done.

Hustle is getting the order because you got there first, or stayed with it after everyone else gave up.

Hustle is shoe leather and elbow grease and sweat and missing lunch.

Hustle is getting prospects to say "yes" after they've said "no" twenty times.

Hustle is doing more for customers than the other person is doing for them.

Hustle is believing in yourself and the business you're in.

Hustle is the sheer joy of winning.

Hustle is being the sorest loser in town.

Hustle is hating to take a vacation because you might miss a piece of the action.

Hustle is heaven if you're a hustler.

Hustle is hell if you're not.

If You Keep Your Nose

If you keep your nose
   on the grindstone rough,
and you keep it down there long enough,

In time you'll forget there are such things
as brooks that babble and birds that sing.

And these three things
   will your world compose:

      Yourself,
      your grindstone,
      and your poor old nose.

ᐓ Enos Mills

Success

To laugh often and love much;
To win the respect of intelligent people
    and the affection of children;
To earn the approbation of honest critics
    and endure the betrayal of false friends;
To appreciate beauty;
To find the best in others;
To leave the world a bit better,
    whether by a healthy child,
    a redeemed social condition,
    or a job well done;
To have played and worked with enthusiasm
    and sung with exultation;
To know even one life has breathed easier
    because you have lived—

This is to have succeeded.

                             ◢ RALPH WALDO EMERSON

When Nothing Seems to Help

When nothing seems to help,
I go and look at a stonecutter
hammering away at his rock
perhaps a hundred times
without as much as a crack showing in it.

Yet at the hundred and first blow
it will split in two,
and I know it was not that blow that did it—
but all that had gone before.

&ও JACOB RIIS

They May Sound Your Praise

They may sound your praise
                     and call you great.
They may single you out for fame.
But you must work with your running mate
Or you'll never win the game;

Oh, never the work of life is done
By the one with a selfish dream,
For the battle is lost or the battle is won
By the spirit of the team.

It's all very well to have courage and skill
And it's fine to be counted a star,
But the single deed with its touch of thrill
Doesn't tell who you are;

For there's no lone hand in the game we play.
We must work to a bigger scheme.
And the thing that counts in the world today
Is, How do you pull with the team?

You may think it fine to be praised for skill,
But a greater thing to do
Is to set your mind and set your will
On the goal that's just in view;

It's helping your teammates to score
When their chances hopeless seem;
It's forgetting self till the game is o'er
And fighting for the team.

Press On

Nothing in the world can take the place
of persistence.

*   Talent will not;
    Nothing is more common than
    unsuccessful people with talent.

*   Genius will not;
    Unrewarded genius is almost a proverb.

*   Education will not;
    The world is full of educated derelicts.

Persistence and determination alone
are omnipotent.

&⁊ CALVIN COOLIDGE

The Winds of Fate

One ship drives East and one drives West
　　With the self-same winds that blow.
'Tis the set of the sails and not the gales
　　Which tells us the way to go.

Like the winds of the sea are the ways of fate,
　　As we voyage along through life.
'Tis the set of the soul that decides its goal,
　　And not the calm or the strife.

ᨔ ELLA WHEELER WILCOX

Don't Quit

When things go wrong,
    as they sometimes will,
When the road you're trudging
    seems all uphill,
When the funds are low,
    and the debts are high,
And you want to smile,
    but you have to sigh.
When care is pressing you down a bit,
Rest if you must—but don't you quit.

Life is queer with its twists and turns,
As every one of us sometimes learns,
And many a failure turns about,
When they might have won
    had they stuck it out.
Don't give up though the pace seems slow—
You may succeed with another blow.

Success is failure turned inside out,
The silver tint of the clouds of doubt,
And you never can tell how close you are,
It may be near when it seems afar,
So stick to the fight when you're hardest hit—
It's when things seem worst,
    That you must not quit.

Guidance

Do Not Follow the Path

Do not follow
   where the path may lead.

Go instead
   where there is no path
     and leave a trail.

Dwell Not on the Past

Dwell not on the past.
    Use it to illustrate a point,
        then leave it behind.
Nothing really matters
    except what you do now
        in this instant of time.

From this moment onward
    you can be an entirely different person,
        filled with love and understanding,
           ready with an outstretched hand,
        uplifted and positive
           in every thought and deed.

                                      ❧ EILEEN CADDY

Great Spirits

Great spirits
   have always encountered
      violent opposition
         from mediocre minds.

ta ALBERT EINSTEIN

On Worry

If you were to read everything
that has ever been written about worry
by the great philosophers of the universe,
you would never read anything
more profound than:

   "Don't cross your bridges
      until you come to them."

and

   "Don't cry over spilt milk."

ta DALE CARNEGIE

Face Your Deficiencies

Face your deficiencies
    and acknowledge them;
    but do not let them master you.
Let them teach you patience,
    sweetness, insight.

True education combines intellect,
    beauty, goodness,
    and the greatest of these is goodness.

When we do the best that we can,
    we never know what miracle is
    wrought in our life,
    or in the life of another.

ð HELEN KELLER

My Highest Aspirations

Far away there in the sunshine
    are my highest aspirations.

I may not reach them,
    but I can look up and
    see their beauty,
    believe in them, and
    try to follow where they lead.

                      ❧ Louisa May Alcott

Live Your Life Each Day

Live your life each day
    as you would climb a mountain.

An occasional glance toward the summit
    keeps the goal in mind,
    but many beautiful scenes are to be
    observed from each new vantage point.

Climb slowly, steadily,
    enjoying each passing moment;
And the view from the summit will serve as
    a fitting climax for the journey.

❦ HAROLD V. MELCHERT

Make No Little Plans

Make no little plans;
They have no magic to stir anyone's blood
And probably themselves
Will not be realized.

Make big plans;
Aim high in hope and work,
Remembering that a noble, logical diagram
Once recorded will not die.

&❧ DANIEL H. BURNHAM

To Thine Own Self Be True

And these few precepts in thy memory
See thou character...

Be thou familiar, but by no means vulgar.
The friends thou hast,
                    and their adoption tried,
Grapple them to thy soul with hoops of steel;
But do not dull thy palm with entertainment
Of each new-hatched, unfledged comrade.

Beware of entrance to a quarrel; But being in,
Bear it that the opposed may beware of thee.

Give everyone thine ear, but few thy voice;
Take each one's censure,
but reserve thy judgment.

Costly thy habit as thy purse can buy,
But not expressed in fancy; rich, not gaudy;
For the apparel oft proclaims the person.

Neither a borrower nor a lender be;
For loan oft loses both itself and friend,
And borrowing dulls the edge of frugality.

This above all—to thine own self be true,
And it must follow as the night the day,
Thou canst not then be false to anyone.

        WILLIAM SHAKESPEARE

Whenever You Are to Do a Thing

Whenever you are to do a thing,
   though it can never be known
   but to yourself,

Ask yourself how you would act
   were all the world looking at you,
   and act accordingly.

&❧ THOMAS JEFFERSON

If You Can't Be a Pine

If you can't be a pine on the top of the hill,
    Be a scrub in the valley—but be
The best little scrub by the side of the hill;
    Be a bush, if you can't be a tree.

If you can't be a bush, be a bit of the grass,
    And some highway happier make;
If you can't be a muskie, then just be a bass—
    But the liveliest bass in the lake.

We can't all be captains, we've got to be crew,
    There's something for all of us here.
There's big work to do and there's lesser to do
    And the task we must do is the near.

If you can't be a highway, then just be a trail,
    If you can't be the sun, be a star;
It isn't by size that you win or you fail—
    Be the best of whatever you are.

⁂ Douglas Malloch

Do Not Stand At My Grave and Weep

Do not stand at my grave and weep.

I am not there. I do not sleep.
I am a thousand winds that blow.
I am the diamond glints on snow.
I am the sunlight on ripened grain.
I am the gentle autumn's rain.

When you waken in the morning's hush,
I am the swift uplifting rush
    of quiet birds in circled flight.
I am the soft stars that shine at night.

Do not stand at my grave and cry;
I am not there. I did not die.

Spiritual Sayings

Ask, and It Shall Be Given

ASK,
and it shall be given to you;

SEEK,
and ye shall find;

KNOCK,
and it shall be opened unto you.

&❧ MATTHEW 7:7

What You Are

What you are
   is God's gift to you;

What you make of yourself
   is your gift to God.

The 23rd Psalm

The Lord is my shepherd;
    I shall not want.
He makes me lie down in green pastures;
He leads me beside still waters;
He restores my soul;
He leads me in the paths of righteousness
    for His name's sake.

Yea though I walk through the
    valley of the shadow of death,
    I will fear no evil:
For Thou art with me;
Thy rod and Thy staff, they comfort me.

Thou preparest a table before me
    in the presence of mine enemies;
Thou anointest my head with oil;
My cup runneth over.

Surely goodness and mercy shall follow me
    all the days of my life;
And I will dwell
    in the house of the Lord forever.

                                  ই PSALM 23

Irish Blessing

May the road rise to meet you,
May the wind be always at your back,

May the sun shine warm upon your face,
May the rains fall soft upon your fields,

And, until we meet again,
May God hold you in the palm of His hand.

Serenity Prayer

GOD grant me the

SERENITY
   to accept the things I cannot change,

COURAGE
   to change the things I can, and

WISDOM
   to know the difference.

                          ❧ REINHOLD NIEBUHR

Song of the Sky Loom

O our Mother the Earth,
                     O our Father the Sky,
Your children are we, and with tired backs
We bring you the gifts you love.
Then weave for us a garment of brightness;

May the warp be the white light of morning,
May the weft be the red light of evening,
May the fringes be the falling rain,
May the border be the standing rainbow.

Thus weave for us a garment of brightness,
That we may walk fittingly where birds sing,
That we may walk fittingly
                     where grass is green,
O our Mother the Earth,
                     O our Father the Sky.

                              ⋙ TEWA

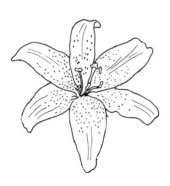

The Prayer of St. Francis

Lord, make me an instrument of Thy peace;
Where there is hatred, let me sow love;
Where there is doubt, faith;
Where there is despair, hope;
Where there is darkness, light;
and where there is sadness, joy.

O Divine Master,
    grant that I may not so much seek
to be consoled, as to console;
to be understood, as to understand;
to be loved, as to love;
for it is in giving that we receive,
it is in pardoning that we are pardoned, and
it is in dying that we are born to eternal life.

ও ST. FRANCIS

Footprints

One night I had a dream. I dreamed I was walking along the beach with the Lord. Across the sky flashed scenes from my life. For each scene, I noticed two sets of footprints in the sand: one belonging to me, and the other to the Lord.

When the last scene of my life flashed before me, I looked back at the footprints in the sand. I noticed that many times along the path of my life, there was only one set of footprints. I also noticed that it happened at the very lowest and saddest times in my life.

This really bothered me, and I questioned the Lord about it. "Lord, you said that once I decided to follow you, you'd walk with me all the way. But I have noticed that during the most troublesome times in my life, there is only one set of footprints. I don't understand why when I needed you the most you would leave me."

The Lord replied, "My precious, precious child. I love you and I would never leave you. During your times of trial and suffering, when you see only one set of footprints, it was then that I carried you."

Love Chapter

Love is patient, love is kind.
It does not envy, it does not boast,
it is not proud.

It is not rude, it is not self-seeking,
it is not easily angered,
it keeps no record of wrongs.

Love does not delight in evil but
rejoices with the truth.

It always protects, always trusts,
always hopes, always perseveres.

Love never fails.

જ 1st Corinthians 13:4-8

O Great Spirit

O GREAT SPIRIT,
whose voice I hear in the winds
and whose breath gives life to all the world,
Hear me! I am small and weak.
I need your strength and wisdom.

LET ME WALK IN BEAUTY,
and make my eyes ever
behold the red and purple sunset.

MAKE MY HANDS
respect the things you have made
and my ears sharp to hear your voice.

MAKE ME WISE
so that I may understand the
things you have taught my people.
Let me learn the lessons you have hidden
in every leaf and rock.

I SEEK STRENGTH,
not to be greater than others,
but to fight my greatest enemy—myself.
Make me always ready to come to you with
clean hands and straight eyes.

SO WHEN LIFE FADES,
as the fading sunset,
my spirit may come to you
without shame.

❧ OGLALA SIOUX

Desiderata

Go placidly amid the noise & haste & remember what peace there may be in silence. As far as possible without surrender, be on good terms with all persons. Speak your truth quietly & clearly; and listen to others, even the dull & ignorant; they too have their story. ❧ Avoid loud & aggressive persons, they are vexations to the spirit. If you compare yourself with others, you may become vain & bitter; for always there will be greater & lesser persons than yourself. Enjoy your achievements as well as your plans. ❧ Keep interested in your own career, however humble; it is a real possession in the changing fortunes of time. Exercise caution in your business affairs; for the world is full of trickery. But let this not blind you to what virtue there is; many persons strive for high ideals; and everywhere life is full of heroism. ❧ Be yourself. Especially do not feign affection. Neither be cynical about love; for in the face of all aridity & disenchantment it is perennial as the grass. ❧ Take kindly the counsel of the years, gracefully surrendering the things of youth. Nurture strength of spirit to shield you in sudden misfortune. But do not distress yourself with imaginings. Many fears are born of fatigue & loneliness. Beyond a wholesome discipline, be gentle with yourself. ❧ You are a child of the universe, no less than the trees & the stars; you have a right to be here. And whether or not it is clear to you, no doubt the universe is unfolding as it should. ❧ Therefore be at peace with God, whatever you conceive Him to be, and whatever your labors & aspirations, in the noisy confusion of life, keep peace with your soul. ❧ With all its sham, drudgery & broken dreams, it is still a beautiful world. Be cheerful. Strive to be happy.

❧ Found in Old Saint Paul's Church, Baltimore; Dated 1692

Rewards

Circumstances

The people who get on in this world
are the people who get up and
look for the circumstances they want,
and if they can't find them,
make them.

⪧ GEORGE BERNARD SHAW

If

If you can keep your head when all about you
Are losing theirs and blaming it on you;
If you can trust yourself when all people doubt you,
But make allowance for their doubting too:
If you can wait and not be tired by waiting,
Or, being lied about, don't deal in lies,
Or, being hated, don't give way to hating,
And yet don't look too good, nor talk too wise;

If you can dream—and not make dreams your master;
If you can think—and not make thoughts your aim,
If you can meet with Triumph and Disaster
And treat those two impostors just the same:
If you can bear to hear the truth you've spoken
Twisted by knaves to make a trap for fools,
Or watch the things you gave your life to, broken,
And stoop and build'em up with worn-out tools;

If you can make one heap of all your winnings
And risk it on one turn of pitch-and-toss,
And lose, and start again at your beginnings,
And never breathe a word about your loss:
If you can force your heart and nerve and sinew
To serve your turn long after they are gone,
And so hold on when there is nothing in you
Except the Will which says to them: "Hold on!"

If you can talk with crowds and keep your virtue,
Or walk with Kings, nor lose the common touch,
If neither foes nor loving friends can hurt you,
If all people count with you, but none too much:
If you can fill the unforgiving minute
With sixty seconds' worth of distance run,
Yours is the Earth and everything that's in it,
And—which is more—you'll be grown up, my child!

&. RUDYARD KIPLING

Children Learn What They Live

Children who live with:

Criticism,
        learn to condemn.
Hostility,
        learn to fight.
Abuse,
        learn to hurt others.
Ridicule,
        learn to be shy.
Shame,
        learn to feel guilty.

Encouragement,
        learn to be confident.
Praise,
        learn to appreciate.
Justice,
        learn to be fair.
Tolerance,
        learn to be patient.
Security,
        learn to have faith.
Approval,
        learn to like themselves.
Acceptance and friendship,
        learn to find love in the world.

DOROTHY LAW NOLTE

I Do the Best I Know How

I do the best I know how,
the very best I can;
and I mean to keep on doing it to the end.

If the end brings me out all right,
what is said against me
will not amount to anything.

If the end brings me out wrong,
ten legions of angels swearing I was right
would make no difference.

           ABRAHAM LINCOLN

Give Someone a Fish

Give someone a fish
    and they're fed for a day.

Teach someone to fish
    and they're fed for a lifetime.

If You Wish to See the Valleys

If you wish to see the valleys,
    climb to the mountain top;
If you desire to see the mountain top,
    rise into the cloud;
But if you seek to understand the cloud,
    close your eyes and think.

❧ KAHLIL GIBRAN

High Flight

Oh, I have slipped the surly bonds of earth,
And danced the skies
           on laughter-silvered wings;
Sunward I've climbed
           and joined the tumbling mirth
Of sun-split clouds—
           and done a hundred things
You have not dreamed of—
           wheeled and soared and swung
High in the sunlit silence. Hov'ring there
I've chased the shouting
           wind along and flung
My eager craft through footless halls of air.
Up, up the long delirious burning blue
I've topped the wind-swept heights
           with easy grace,
Where never lark, or even eagle flew;
And, while with silent, lifting mind I've trod
The high untrespassed sanctity of space,
Put out my hand,
           and touched the face of God.

            JOHN GILLESPIE MAGEE, JR.

Not in Vain

If I can stop one heart from breaking,
I shall not live in vain;
If I can ease one life the aching,
Or cool one pain,
Or help one fainting robin
Unto his nest again,
I shall not live in vain.

ào EMILY DICKINSON

Most Beautiful Compensations

It is one of the most beautiful
compensations of this life
that you cannot sincerely try
to help another
without helping yourself.

ào RALPH WALDO EMERSON

If You Think You Are

If you think you are beaten,
    you are;
If you think you dare not,
    you don't.
If you'd like to win,
    but think you can't,
    it's almost a cinch you won't.

If you think you'll lose, you're lost;
    For out in the world we find
Success begins with a person's will:
    It's all in the state of mind.

Life's battles don't always go
    to the stronger or faster one;
But sooner or later the ones who win
    are the ones who think they can.

If You Are a Streetsweeper

If you are called to be a streetsweeper,
you should sweep streets
  even as Michelangelo painted,
  or Beethoven composed music,
  or Shakespeare wrote poetry.

You should sweep streets so well that all the
hosts of heaven and earth will pause to say:
  "Here lived a great streetsweeper
  who did the job well."

         ɛ͡ MARTIN LUTHER KING, JR.

Life's Mirror

There are loyal hearts, there are spirits brave,
There are souls that are pure and true;
Then give to the world the best you have,
And the best will come back to you.

Give love, and love to your life will flow,
A strength in your utmost need;
Have faith, and a score of hearts will show
Their faith in your work and deed.

Give truth, and your gift will be paid in kind,
And honor will honor meet;
And the smile which is sweet will surely find
A smile that is just as sweet.

Give sorrow and pity to those who mourn;
You will gather in flowers again
The scattered seeds from your thought outborne
Though the sowing seemed but vain.

For life is the mirror of king and slave,
'Tis just what we are and do;
Then give to the world the best you have
And the best will come back to you.

                 ❧ MADELINE S. BRIDGES

Take Time

Take time to work—
        it is the price of success.
Take time to think—
        it is the source of power.
Take time to read—
        it is the foundation of wisdom.

Take time to play—
        it is the secret of staying young.
Take time to be quiet—
        it is the opportunity to seek God.

Take time to be aware—
        it is the opportunity to help others.
Take time to love and be loved—
        it is the nourishment of the soul.

Take time to laugh—
        it is the music of the heart.
Take time to be friendly—
        it is the road to happiness.

Take time to dream—
        it is what the future is made of.
Take time to pray—
        it is the greatest power on earth.

There is a time for everything...

Something Beautiful Remains

The tide recedes
   but leaves behind
      bright seashells on the sand.

The sun goes down,
   but gentle warmth
      still lingers on the land.

The music stops,
   and yet it echoes on
      in sweet refrains...

For every joy
   that passes,
      something beautiful remains.

About the Editor

Marty Maskall has been collecting inspiring quotations for the past 30 years. She believes strongly in the benefits of positive thinking.

Marty is the daughter of an English teacher who taught her to love the beauty and power of words. She was trained in biology and zoology (B.A. from Stanford and M.A. from Duke). Computers fascinated her, so she decided to be a programmer. In 1983 she changed to executive recruiting, and she now finds people for jobs in the information processing field. Her business, Marty Maskall & Associates, is based in Fair Oaks, California.

In her spare time, Marty enjoys hiking, ballroom dancing, and Toastmasters International. She is also a Big Sister and a member of Optimist International, Data Processing Management Association, National Association for Professional Saleswomen, Business and Professional Women, National Organization for Women, Mensa, and the Sierra Club. She organized the Towe Ford Museum Speakers Bureau. She has a Distinguished Toastmaster designation and a Certificate in Data Processing, and she is listed in Who's Who in the West. This is her first book.

Bibliography

Grateful acknowledgement is given to the original authors of these works, even if they are anonymous. Where the author is not designated in the text, the author is unknown. Diligent attempts have been made to trace the source of the passages and to give proper credit. If there are errors, they will gladly be corrected in the next edition, provided that written notification is received by the publisher.

Some passages have been adapted to eliminate sexist language and are so noted by the word "adapted" in the list below. For rewording, I have used guidelines suggested by Casey Miller and Kate Swift in their *Handbook of Nonsexist Writing*, (New York, NY: Harper & Row, 1988).

The beautiful line drawings used for the illustrations have been taken from:

Tarbox, Charlene, *Floral Designs and Motifs for Artists, Needleworkers, and Craftspeople* (New York, NY: Dover Publications, Inc., 1984), pp. 5 (narcissus), 8 (impatiens), 18 (lily), 20 (tulip), 23 (rose), 28 (pansy), 31 (rose), 60 (dogwood), 74 (anemone), and 77 (daffodil). Used by permission.

The authors and the reference to their quotation(s) are listed below:

Addison, Joseph
    p. 6   Friendship improves happiness
Alcoholics Anonymous
    p. 30   Just for Today. See Sybyl Partridge.
Alcott, Louisa May
    p. 64   My Highest Aspirations

Fulghum, Robert
    p. 42   All I Really Need to Know. *All I Really Need to Know I Learned in Kindergarten.* New York, NY: Random House, 1986, 1988. Reprinted by permission of Villard Books, a division of Random House, Inc.

Gawain, Shakti
    p. 14   The Most Powerful Thing You Can Do. *Creative Visualization.*

Gibran, Kahlil
    p. 86   If You Wish to See the Valleys. *Spiritual Sayings of Kahlil Gibran.* New York, NY: Citadel Press, Inc., 1962 by Anthony Ferris.

Goddard, Robert
    p. 50   The Impossible

Goethe, Johann W.
    p. 47   Commitment. Adapted.

Hawthorne, Nathaniel
    p. 2   Happiness

Holz, Brian C.
    p. 37   Believe in Yourself. Used by permission.

Jackson, Andrew
    p. 28   One Person with Courage. Adapted.

Jefferson, Thomas
    p. 68   Whenever You Are to Do a Thing

Kaiser, Henry
    p. 41   Problems Are Opportunities

Kalidasa
    p. 15   Look to This Day. From the Sanskrit.

Keller, Helen
    p. 63   Face Your Deficiencies

King, Martin Luther
    p. 90   If You Are a Streetsweeper. Adapted.

Kipling, Rudyard
    p. 83   If. *Rewards and Fairies.* England, 1910. Adapted.

Lao Tsu
    p. 28   The Journey of a Thousand Miles

Lincoln, Abraham
    p. 44   Things May Come
    p. 85   I Do the Best I Know How

Lyons, Kay
    p. 44   Yesterday, Tomorrow, Today

Tewa

p. 75   Song of the Sky Loom. *Songs of the Tewa.* New York: Exposition of Indian Tribal Arts, 1933. Edited and translated by Herbert J. Spinden.

Thompson, Dorothy

p. 26   No Longer Afraid

Thoreau, Henry David

p. 48   Castles in the Air. Adapted.

Waitley, Denis

p. 41   Life Is the Movie You See. *The Winner's Edge.* New York, NY: Times Books, a division of Random House, Inc., 1980.

White, William Allen

p. 4   Do Not Fear Tomorrow

Wilcox, Ella Wheeler

p. 57   The Winds of Fate

Wordsworth, William

p. 3 A Host of Golden Daffodils. *Poems in Two Volumes.* England, 1807.

Many of the quotations were found in other publications, and no source was indicated or could be found. I am grateful for the use of the books listed below. The reader may also wish to consult these beautiful books.

Allen, Charles L. *Home Fires: A Treasury of Wit and Wisdom.* Waco, TX: World Books, 1987.

Great Quotations, Publisher, Lombard, Illinois:
The Best of Success, Compiled by Wynn Davis
Commitment to Excellence
Motivational Quotes

Hayward, Susan. *A Guide for the Advanced Soul: A Book of Insight.* Crows Nest, NSW, Australia: In-Tune Books, 1984.

James, Jennifer. *Success is the Quality of the Journey.* New York, NY: Newmarket Press, 1983.

Look to This Day. Kansas City, MO: Hallmark Cards, Inc., 1975.

Manager's Inspirational Quotations: A Treasury of Inspirational Quotations for the Business Person. Garden City, NY: Dale Carnegie & Associates, Inc., 1984.

Michael, Gloria. *Coupons of Hope.* Los Angeles, CA: City of Hope, 1989.

Otis, Harry B. *The Best of the Cockle Bur.* Omaha, NE: The Bur, Inc., 1987.

Petty, Jo. *Apples of Gold.* Norwalk, CT: C. R. Gibson Company, 1962.

Watson, Lillian Eichler. *Light from Many Lamps.* New York, NY: Simon & Schuster, Inc., 1951.

Index of Authors

Index of Titles

Your Favorite Quotes

Your Feedback is Requested

Now that you have had a chance to make friends with *The Attitude Treasury*, please write me and tell me how you use the book, and share your suggestions for the next edition. Do you have any favorite quotes not included here? Please send them to me with the source (if you know it).

Send your suggestions to:

Marty Maskall
The Attitude Works Publishing Company
8456 Hidden Valley Circle
Fair Oaks, CA 95628

You may copy the order form on the last page so that you can share *The Attitude Treasury* with your friends.

To Order

To order additional copies of *The Attitude Treasury*, please send your name, address, daytime phone number, and a check payable to:

The Attitude Works Publishing Company
8456B Hidden Valley Circle
Fair Oaks, CA 95628
(916) 967-2470

When you order:	The price is:
1 - 4 books	$9.95 each
5 - 9	$8.95 each
10 - 24	$7.95 each
25 +	$6.95 each

Sales tax:
Please add applicable sales tax for books shipped to California addresses.

Shipping:
$2 for shipping via U.S. mail book rate, or
$4 for United Parcel Service,
plus 50 cents for each additional book.

Allow 3 weeks for book rate and 10 days for UPS.